A Perfect Day in Lebanon
Published by Olive Tree Press, 2024

Text and Illustrations Copyright © 2024, Mona Mortazavi

Illustrated in Watercolor

Olive Tree Press
Houston, Texas
www.olivetreepressco.com

ISBN: 978-1-965289-01-3 Paperback
ISBN: 978-1-965289-02-0 Hardcover

To all the little explorers out there — may you always see the world with wonder and an open heart.

A Perfect Day
in Lebanon

Written & Illustrated by
Mona Mortazavi

Lebanon is a small, mountainous country on the eastern shore of the Mediterranean Sea in the Middle East.

Many things make Lebanon special — ancient Roman ruins, limestone caves, historic churches and mosques, beautiful beaches, delicious food, and welcoming mountain villages.

You can drive from the north of Lebanon to the south in just about three hours!

Some of the earliest human settlements in the world existed in Lebanon. Long ago, the cities of Tyre, Sidon, and Byblos were busy centers of trade for the Phoenicians.

In Lebanon, many people speak three languages — Arabic, French, and English. You'll even see street signs written in all three!

The capital is Beirut, located in the center of the country along the Mediterranean Sea.

Let's imagine a perfect day together in Lebanon!

Start in Beirut with a traditional Lebanese breakfast of fool (fava beans) with tomatoes, parsley, and olive oil, and a manoushe (flatbread with cheese or herbs).

Then go to a dekene (local grocery store) for some candy and juice.

Take a taxi to the Raouché, a long sidewalk by the sea.

On your walk, swing by a street cart to buy some Lebanese bread called ka'ak. This savory bread is covered in sesame seeds — crispy on the outside, soft and chewy on the inside.

Stop by Pigeon Rock to admire the view of the large
rock formations in the sparkling water.

Visit the central square downtown to see the famous clock tower.

And have some yummy booza (ice cream)!

Explore the Beirut Souks Mall downtown, where shops, cafes, and a unique blend of old and new architecture come together in one place.

Go hiking in the majestic Cedars of God forest, where you can see Lebanon's national tree — the cedar — which is proudly featured on the Lebanese flag.

Visit the Sidon Sea Castle in the port city of Sidon.

The castle was built in the 13th century by the Crusaders as a fortress.

Go to the beach in Batroun and cool off with a sweet slice of watermelon.

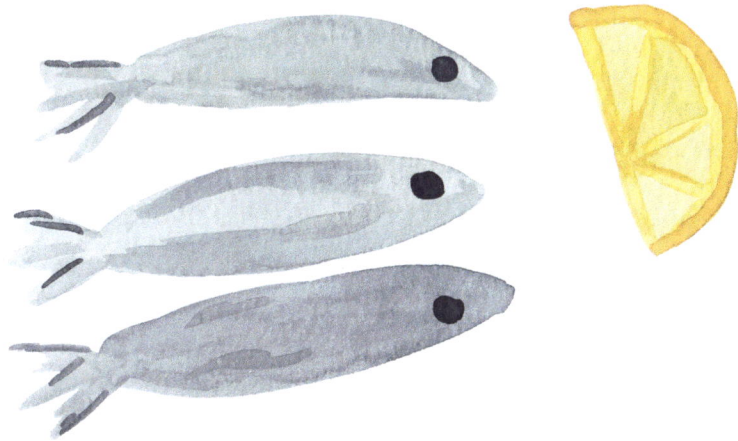

Enjoy some fresh sardines at a restaurant by the beach.

Or go explore the Roman ruins in Baalbek, where towering stone columns have stood for thousands of years.

Or take a stroll through the souk (marketplace) in Byblos, where you can shop for souvenirs and explore one of the world's oldest cities.

Or go to Jounieh and ride the téléférique cable car all the way up the mountain for an amazing view of the sea and city below.

Or go to Beiteddine to see the historic 18th-century Beiteddine Palace, filled with arches, courtyards, and colorful mosaics.

Visit a village home in the mountains and play in the garden.

While you're there, pick some juicy grapes straight from the vine to eat.

Before the day ends, enjoy a delicious dinner of kibbeh (ground beef and bulgur wheat), warak enab (grape leaves stuffed with meat and rice), and hummus (a creamy blend of chickpeas and tahini).

The day is over. Let's have fun again tomorrow!

Now it's your turn — what does *your* perfect day in Lebanon look like?

ABOUT THE AUTHOR & ILLUSTRATOR

This book was written and illustrated by Mona Mortazavi, who drew inspiration for A Perfect Day in Lebanon from her many childhood summers spent there. Some of her favorite memories include breakfasts at her grandparents' home in Beirut and playing in her family's village garden.

As a mother, Mona believes that stories can build bridges, spark imagination, and create a sense of belonging. She hopes this book inspires children to dream up their own perfect day in Lebanon — and brings joy to anyone who holds Lebanon close to their heart.

A NOTE FROM THE AUTHOR

If A Perfect Day in Lebanon made you smile, please consider leaving a review on Amazon — your feedback helps others discover this book and supports my small business!

To explore more of my children's books and coloring books, visit my Amazon author page or follow along on Instagram @olivetreepressco for updates, behind-the-scenes art, and new releases.

www.ingramcontent.com/pod-product-compliance
Lightning Source LLC
Chambersburg PA
CBHW061143030426
42335CB00002B/87